EARLY INTERMEDIATE

ACCENTS AROUND THE WORLD

10 ORIGINAL PIANO PIECES BY
WILLIAM GILLOCK

ISBN 978-1-4803-5429-6

WILLIS MUSIC

EXCLUSIVELY DISTRIBUTED BY

HAL•LEONARD®
CORPORATION
7777 W. BLUEMOUND RD. P.O. BOX 13819 MILWAUKEE, WI 53213

Visit Hal Leonard Online at
www.halleonard.com

CONTENTS

NOTE: Countries/regions are suggestions.

American Folk Dance

William Gillock

Lively, with simple rhythmic directness

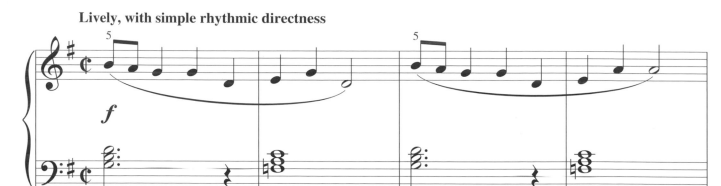

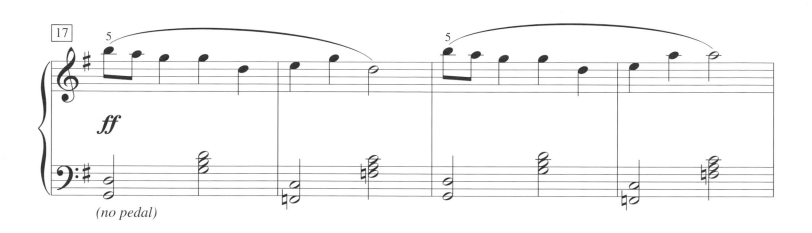

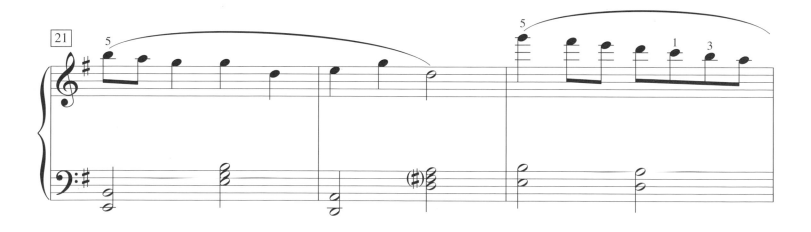

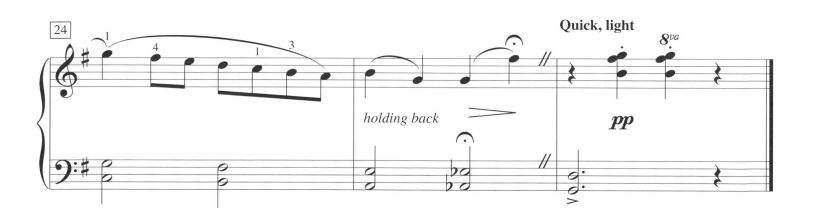

Arabian Nights

William Gillock

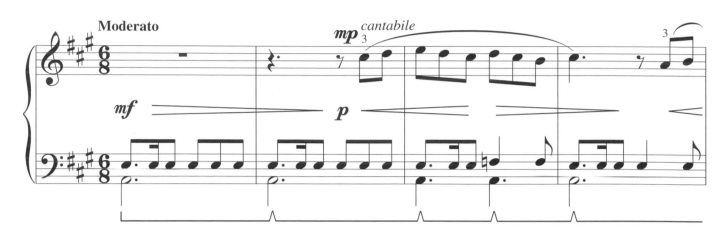

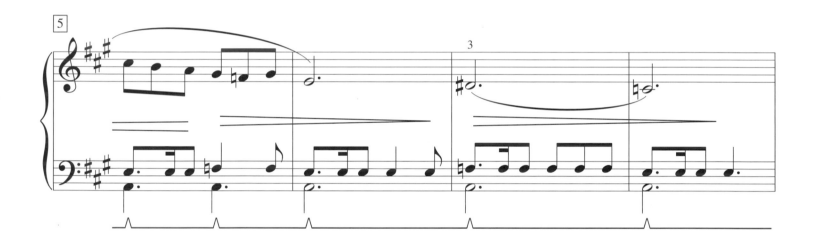

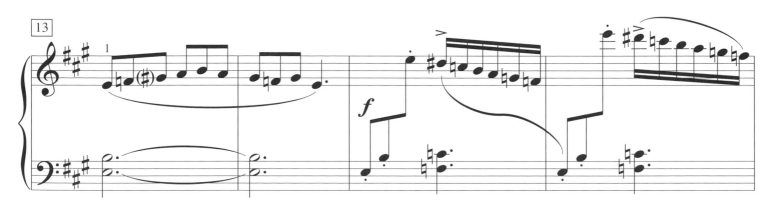

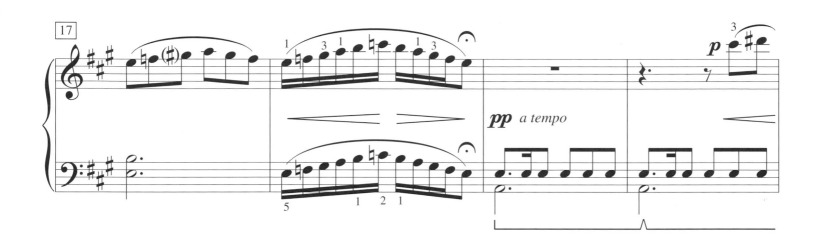

Carnival in Rio

William Gillock

Tempo di Samba

A Highland Ballad

William Gillock

In Old Vienna

Tempo di valse Viennese

William Gillock

Land of Pharaoh

William Gillock

Mazurka

William Gillock

A Memory of Paris

William Gillock

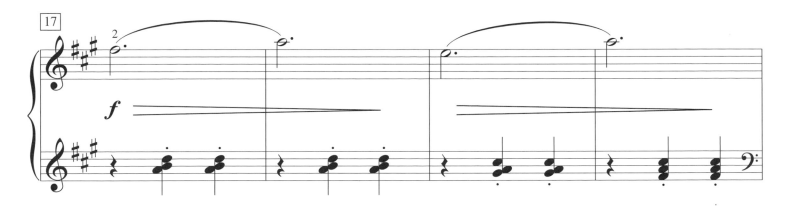

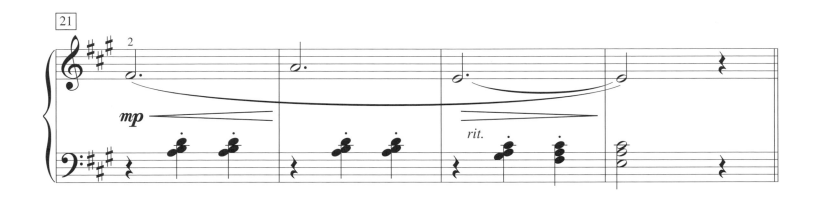

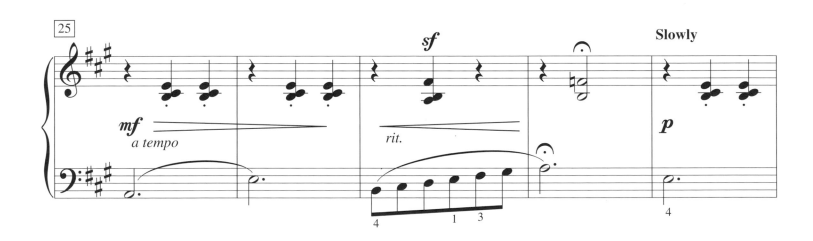

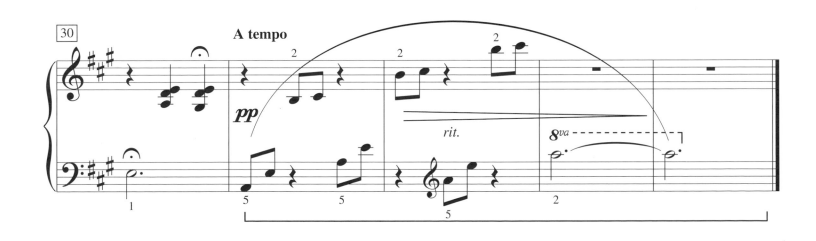

To Mildred R. Dalton

Sarabande

William Gillock

*Accompaniment portato throughout.

Spanish Gypsies

William Gillock

Flamenco style; intensely rhythmic

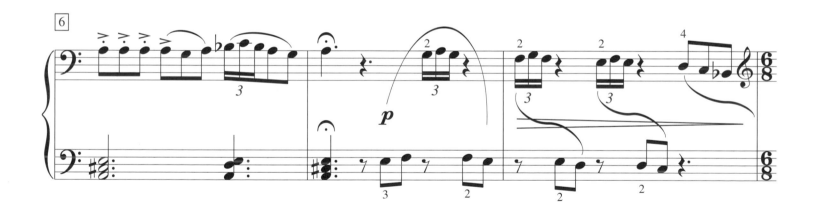

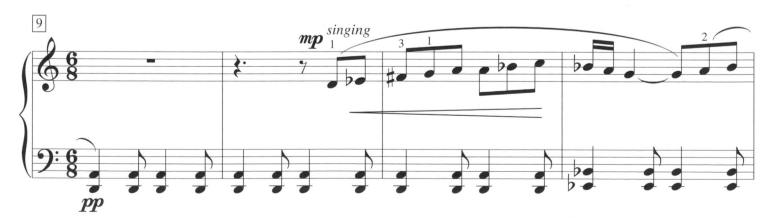

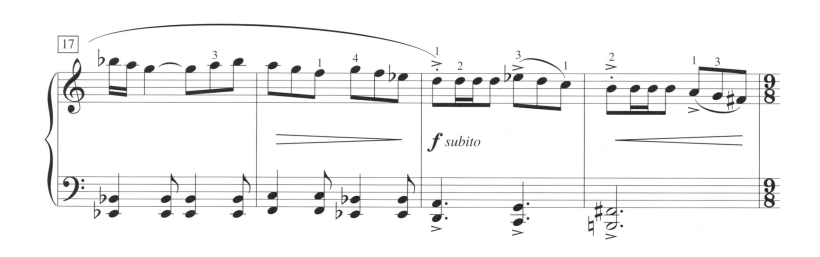

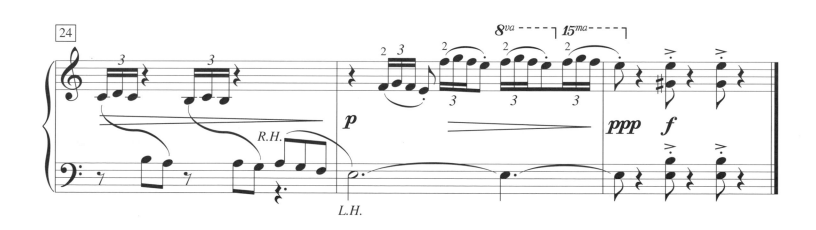

WILLIAM LAWSON GILLOCK

Beloved composer William Lawson Gillock was born in La Russell, Missouri on July 1, 1917. His father, a dentist, was also a musician who played by ear, and undoubtedly influenced his son's love for the piano. There was no piano teacher in the little town of La Russell, and at age 6, Gillock began weekly piano lessons 15 miles away—an extensive distance in the 1920s. Nevertheless, when he went to college, he was hesitant about pursuing a career in music and instead pursued and obtained a degree in art from Central Methodist College. However, his piano and composition teacher at CMC, Dr. N. Louise Wright, recognized his talents and encouraged him to write piano literature specifically for children. Thankfully, he took this advice and thus began his illustrious career as a composer.

Gillock moved to New Orleans in 1943, and the distinctive Southern city would inspire many compositions, including his popular *New Orleans Jazz Styles* books. Gillock also gained respect as a teacher during his tenure in Louisiana, maintaining a studio for almost 30 years. He moved to Dallas, Texas in 1970 where he remained in high demand as a clinician, adjudicator, and composer until his death in 1993.

Affectionately called "the Schubert of children's composers" in tribute to his extraordinary melodic gift, Gillock's numerous piano solos and ensembles exude a special warmth and sophistication. William Gillock was honored on multiple occasions by the National Federation of Music Clubs (NFMC) with the Award of Merit for Service to American Music, and he lives on through his music, which remains immensely popular in the United States, Canada, Japan, and throughout the world.